Hippopotamus Dancing and other poems

Brian Moses

CAMBRIDGE
UNIVERSITY PRESS

For my daughters, Karen and Linette

Published by the Press Syndicate of the University of Cambridge
The Pitt Building, Trumpington Street, Cambridge CB2 1RP
40 West 20th Street, New York, NY 10011–4211, USA
10 Stamford Road, Oakleigh, Melbourne 3166, Australia

First published 1994

Printed in Great Britain at the University Press, Cambridge

A catalogue record for this book is available from the British Library

Library of Congress cataloguing in publication data applied for

ISBN 0 521 44141 2 hardback
ISBN 0 521 44684 8 paperback

Cover and text illustration by Frank James

Project editor: Claire Llewellyn

VN

Contents

My sister said . . .

Have you ever been called a "little beast"? Some people think of children in this way!

This poem was written after a visit to a classroom where "little beasts" were studying minibeasts. I thought about all the awful things a sister might do with these creatures when she was trying to be beastly!

My sister said,
"If you do that to me again,
I'll put . . .

"slugs down your dress,
spiders in your vest,
earwigs in your ear
and caterpillars in your cornflakes.

"I'll put . . .
beetles between your sheets,
squirmy worms in your hair,
centipedes in your lunchbox
and grasshoppers (real whoppers) in your slippers.

"I'll put . . .
ants in your knickers,
bugs under your pillow,
snails in your school bag
and nits in your nightgown.

"I'll really make you scream," she said,
"you'll yell and shake and shiver."
And I know that she will,
and I promise I won't . . . NOT EVER!

Somebody else

Have you ever dreamed of being somebody famous, or just someone
else in your class? If you think somebody else is always having a
better time than you, then this poem is about that feeling.

Who is this somebody else,
who always seems to be
out there, somewhere, some place,
having more fun than me?

Has somebody else got a name,
does she live with her mum and dad,
does she go to bed at the proper time
and is she ever bad?

Does somebody else get measles
on the day before her birthday?
Does she catch a double dose of flu
when she's Mary in the Christmas play?

Is somebody else ever slapped
for being unkind to her friend,
or sent up early to bed before
her programme comes to an end?

I think I hate her the most
when we're picking teams in games.
"We're having somebody else," they say
and call me awful names.

But when somebody else is in trouble,
it's then I begin to doubt.
Do I really want to change places
now that her luck has run out?

This time

When something like this happens at home, people lose their tempers, the temperature rises, and a lot of energy is used up. When I read this poem out loud, I try to put the same kind of energy into it – I "chase . . . up the stairs", "ROAR like an angry bear", and shout like Dad.

I'm always doing things wrong,
I never get them right.
My sister always laughs
and that's when we start to fight.
We wrestle in the living room,
I chase her up the stairs,
she flings the door in my face
and I ROAR like an angry bear.
Inside her room she's hiding
but I know just where she'll be,
crouched inside her wardrobe
waiting to jump out on me.
Then Dad calls out, "If you can't behave,
I've told you what we'll do:
we'll go away for a holiday
and we won't be taking you.
Your Mum and I are tired
of your squabbles around the home.
If we leave you here together,
you'll have to get by on your own."
My sister comes out of the wardrobe
and we kneel by the bedroom door:
"Do you think they really mean it?"
"I don't know, I couldn't be sure."
"If you think we don't really mean it,"
Dad shouts, "then just you step out of line."
We look at each other, both thinking the same –
they really must mean it, this time!

Photographs

I like to look through old family photographs. Some of mine are almost one hundred years old and show my great-great-grandparents sitting stiff and formal in their best Sunday clothes.

Old photographs of ourselves show just how much we change as the years go by. There are always questions to be asked about photographs, which is why this poem is written for two voices, as a series of questions and answers.

Who's that figure standing there,
slim at the waist, shoulder-length hair?
That's your dad twenty years ago,
wouldn't think so now though.

Who's that young girl skipping high,
caught against a sunny sky?
That's your mum some years ago,
looks a bit different now though.

Who's that tall and lanky lad,
looks a little bit like Dad?
That's his brother, Uncle Joe,
wouldn't know him now though.

Who's that lady by the swing,
practising her curtsying?
That's Auntie many years ago,
she doesn't dance much now though.

Who's that tiny wrinkled baby,
mouth wide open, bawling loudly?
Oh, come on now, surely you know,
you're still a noisy so and so!

The spider under the stairs

I don't mind small spiders, but one day my young daughter Karen
discovered one that was huge, black and hairy. We trapped it in the
cupboard under our stairs, then swept it up in the dustpan and set it
free outside our back door.

I went upstairs to the room where I work, but I couldn't concentrate. I
kept thinking about that spider . . .

In the darkest corner is a pair of eyes
and I'm sure, for certain, they're growing in size
till they seem to say, now just you dare
take one step further and I'll jump in your hair.

So I reach out quickly and grab the broom
but I hear a movement deep in the gloom,
and I feel like St George about to do battle
with my broomstick spear and my sister's rattle!

Then something scuttles from its hiding place
and something sticky trails over my face
as the spider spreads its silky threads,
winding them round and round my head.

And it's coming for me, it's coming now
and I'm shouting, "MUM, PLEASE COME," but the row
her hoover makes is all I can hear
and the noise is pounding in my ears.

If I'm really naughty, Mum says, "Beware,
or I'll open that cupboard under the stairs
and I'll pop you inside and I won't let you out
no matter how loudly you scream or shout."

"Oh, ssssay you wwwouldn't do that," I say,
my eyes full of fright as I back away.
She smiles and says, "No, I don't think I would,
but you can't be sure, so you'd better be good!"

Naming the rabbit

Thinking of a name for a pet can cause any number of arguments. Everyone in the family has to feel that the name is suitable. A name like Fifi might suit a small lap dog but it would sound silly if it were given to a hunting dog! My family argued over a name for our rabbit . . .

"You can't call him Cuddles,"
my dad said to me.
"That rabbit's already
a bit of a bruiser,
looks more like Boris or Horace or Jake,
take your pick,
there are names galore.
What about Bouncer or Thumper or Joe,
how about Biffo or Basher or Rambo?
That bunny's got bounce,
it's plain to see,
in a boxing ring
he'd be heavyweight champ.
But the choice is yours,
call him what you like,
and don't take all night
deciding . . ."
So we called him Cuddles.

Silverfish

When I lived in a house that was built on marshland, I often used to find silverfish in my kitchen. These tiny insects thrive in damp conditions but dislike bright lights. I would often turn on the kitchen light first thing in the morning and glimpse several silverfish scuttling away.

Small reptilian creature,
catching me by surprise.
You sneak about the kitchen
on your nightly exercise.

Then early every morning,
I wonder what you think,
finding that some giant
has trapped you in the sink.

Perhaps I'll run the water
and flush you down the drain,
or launch a rescue mission
with a tiny paper plane.

I think you must party all night
in our kitchen when it's quiet.
I wonder what it sounds like
when silverfish run riot?

Hippopotamus dancing

If ever I visit a zoo, I make straight for the hippos. I love their great
bulk! Although they may be slow and clumsy on land, in the water they
are very skilful. I began to wonder how hippos keep fit. I tried to bring
a jerky rhythm to this poem, which would match the hippos'
movements as they do their workouts.

In the hippo house
at the city zoo,
hippos are moving
to the boogaloo,
big hippos shuffle,
little hippos trot,
everyone giving it
all they've got.

Hip-hippo, hippopotamus dancing,
hip-hippo, hippopotamus dancing.

Every hippo
keeping fit,
fighting the flab,
doing their bit,
weight-training one week,
aerobics another,
tiny hippopotami
move with their mothers.

Hip-hippo, hippopotamus dancing,
hip-hippo, hippopotamus dancing.

Hippos in tutus,
hippos in vests,
baby hippos
doing their best
to keep clear of Dad
as he stumbles around,
causing commotion,
shaking the ground.

Hip-hippo, hippopotamus dancing,
hip-hippo, hippopotamus dancing.

Trouble at the Dinosaur Café

I once visited a school where the theme for their Book Week was Dinosaurs. I was fascinated by dinosaurs when I was young, but hadn't written any poems about them.

I think the idea for this poem came to me, as many do, while I was driving. I wanted to put over the fact that some dinosaurs were plant eaters while others ate meat, and I thought about setting the poem in a café.

Down at the Dinosaur Café
everybody was doing fine.
Steggy was slurping his swamp juice
while Iggy sat down to dine.

Bronto was eating his tree roots
and had ordered vegetable pie,
when in stomped Tyrannosaurus
with a wicked gleam in his eye.

He read the menu from left to right
then gobbled it up in one gulp.
He chewed upon it thoughtfully
as the paper turned to pulp.

"You plant eaters are fine," he said,
"if that's all you want to eat,
but I'm a growing dinosaur
and my stomach cries out for meat.

"I need something extra
to get me through my day.
I do lots of ROARING and BELLOWING,
I just can't get by on hay."

Steggy stiffened, Iggy trembled,
while Bronto fell off his chair.
Tyrannosaurus turned his head
and fixed them with his stare:

"There's nothing I like more," he said,
"than a tasty dinosaur stew,
and for extra special flavour
I'll add **YOU**

and YOU

and **YOU!**"

The grumposaurus

My daughter often wakes up in a grumpy mood. This is usually because she hasn't gone to sleep early enough the night before. I started to tease her by calling her a "grumposaurus". What name would suit you?

Each morning a grumposaurus
tears into our bedroom,
burrows down
beneath the duvet
and roars out commands
most grumposaurusly:
"Where's my drink?"
"I want a story!"

We really have to take care
not to annoy this beast.
We feed her breakfast,
a TV cartoon or two.
Then the grumposaurus
can be quite friendly,
she hugs and smothers us,
tries to mother us . . .

But we never know when
she'll turn grumposaurus.
We never know when,
mouth wide, she'll roar at us,
or sit in a huff
and just ignore us.
It's a tough life
living with a grumposaurus.

Spring in the city

Signs of spring in the countryside are everywhere, but in the city they develop against a background of buildings. One day there's nothing, but the next, a flash of colour, a whirr of wings, a sign that winter's grip is weakening.

Spring has come to the city,
to the streets and the railway line.
Winter is packing its bags,
the sun has begun to shine.

The cherry tree in our garden
wears a wedding dress of white.
Geese are in flight once more,
and days are warm with delight.

There are plenty of baby lambs
to feed at the city farm,
and a single primrose shows its head
at the dump, like a lucky charm.

A heron is raising its young
at the flooded gravel pits,
and the nest box on our garden wall
is a shelter for baby tits.

Wrens are finding new homes
in an untidy, overgrown hedge.
Pigeons keep to their buildings
and jostle for space on a ledge.

Spring has come to the city,
there's a lightness in everyone's tread.
Office workers have shed their coats,
there's a promise of summer ahead.

Trees

From the room in my house where I write most of my poems, I look out on a number of very tall trees. I enjoy looking at them; they were here long before the houses, and are a link with the past landscape. I sometimes wonder how many trees were felled to make room for the houses.

I wrote this poem as a reminder that trees need friends.

Trees are always homes
to every sort of creature.
In an empty landscape
a tree is a special feature.

Trees can be deciduous,
pine trees are coniferous.
Trees will never hurt you,
no tree is carnivorous!

So snuggle up to a sycamore,
cuddle close to a pine,
wrap your arms around an oak,
enjoy a joke with a lime.

A tree will always listen,
tell your troubles to a tree.
To the mystery of life
an ash may hold the key.

So treat a tree politely,
show it you're sincere.
Long after we have disappeared,
trees will still be here.

Wilderness Hill

There's a road in Margate called Wilderness Hill. I noticed the sign and thought that it sounded mysterious and a little scary. I used it as the subject for this poem.

Children never go there
and traffic never slows
on Wilderness Hill.

Winds blow cold there
and stories are told
about Wilderness Hill.

Birds never call there,
avoided by all
is Wilderness Hill.

Now flowers never grow there,
and everyone knows
about Wilderness Hill.

Do you?

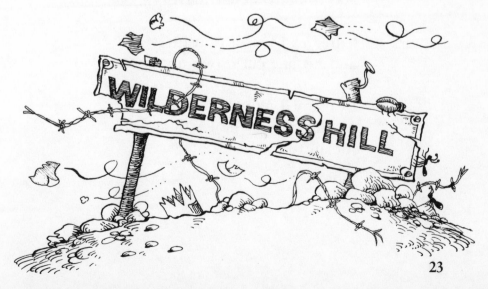

Dreamer

A dream can be crazy or frightening, but some dreams are pleasant and as you find yourself waking up, you try to cling on to the dream for just a little while longer.

In this poem I wanted to say something about the world and the way that it is being treated. I thought of all the good things that I'd like to see happen and then used a line that almost repeated itself to give the poem a rhythm.

I dreamt I was an ocean
and no one polluted me.

I dreamt I was a whale
and no hunters chased after me.

I dreamt I was the air
and nothing blackened me.

I dreamt I was a stream
and nobody poisoned me.

I dreamt I was an elephant
and nobody stole my ivory.

I dreamt I was a rain forest
and no one cut down my trees.

I dreamt I painted a smile
on the face of the Earth
for all to see.

Hatching eggs

In a school where I once taught, one of the teachers decided that she'd like her class to watch baby chicks hatching from their eggs.

For three weeks the eggs were cared for until cracks began to appear. Each morning I'd rush in with the children to check what had happened, and I was fortunate enough to be there when one chick pushed its way out. That moment was magical.

Daniel wrote "D" on his egg
and Carly pencilled a "C".
Trish drew a face on hers
but Martin just wrote "Me".

One was left for Emma,
absent with chickenpox.
We placed it with the others
in the incubator box.

"How long will it take," we asked,
"before our chicks are born?"
"Twenty-one days," our teacher said,
"as long as we keep them warm."

We listened every day until
the chicks began to squeak.
A pattern of cracks appeared,
then someone saw a beak!

Our eyes were window wide
as the little chicks broke free.
It wasn't every day we saw
such magic in Class 1B.

Maths is fun

This poem is somewhat tongue in cheek! I love words, but numbers frighten me. I wasn't very good at maths when I was at school but I have since met a number of teachers who can really make maths fun. This poem is dedicated to one of them, Mr Tom Collins.

Maths is fun,
maths is brill,
numbers give me
such a thrill.

I love to get
my figures right,
numbers fill me
with delight.

When the teacher
ticks my work,
I ask for more,
I never shirk

or ever think of
playing about,
I really love
figuring out

the kind of sums
that others hate,
they never get me
in a state.

Oh, I love maths
I really do.
What puzzles me
is why don't you?

First and last

Like "Maths is fun", this poem was written when I was asked for some poems on a maths theme. I remembered how much I'd enjoyed coming first in something when I was a child and how, at other times, I wanted to be last. I decided to write a poem in which these two opposites were repeated line by line.

I'm the last one at school in the morning
and first out the door at night,
I'm the first one in the dinner queue
but the last to get my maths right.

I'm the last to help tidy up
and the first to switch on TV,
I'm the last to get out of bed
and the first to finish my tea.

I'm the last to jump in the water
when we stand at the edge of the pool,
I'm first to the ice-cream van
when it waits outside my school.

I'm the last to finish my homework
and the first to the shop for sweets,
I'm the last to volunteer
but the first in line for treats!

I'm the last to do what I'm told
and it makes my teacher shout,
but if friends of mine are in trouble
I'll be the first to help them out.

Well, what happened?

I used to teach in primary schools, and at one school I was in charge of boys' discipline. This meant that any boys who had been naughty were sent to me.

I often had to listen to both sides of the story after a fight broke out in the playground. Two lads would be standing in front of me, perhaps a little worried about what I might say or do, and I'd always find myself starting off with, "Well, what happened?"

This poem is for two voices. Try reading it with a friend.

"I raised my voice,
he raised his fist.
I called him names,
he twisted my wrist."

"I held his arm,
he kicked my shin.
I said I'd get mad
if he didn't pack it in."

"He pulled my nose,
I belted his ear.
He said you'd better
get out of here."

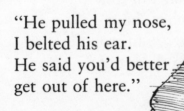

"I told him my brother
would give him a clout.
He said his big sister
would sort me out."

"We argued and fought,
we shouted and swore.
I told him my dad
would give him what for."

"We rolled on the ground,
we clinched and we kicked,
till someone said, 'Watch it,
you'll both be nicked.'"

"And that's when you came, sir,
and pulled us away,
but we're friends again now,
can we go back and play?"

Hands

This poem arose out of something my small daughter said to me.
She'd done something naughty – I can't remember what now – and she
blamed it on her bad hand. "This one's a good hand," she said, "but
this one is the naughty hand."

This hand is a good hand,
it helps me to write.
But this hand is a bad hand,
it gets me into fights.

The good hand is careful,
clever and neat.
The bad hand is naughty,
it slaps and it cheats.

The good hand is never seen
larking about.
The bad hand is always caught
giving a clout.

If I could just turn
my bad hand to good,
then perhaps I'd always
do what I should.

But I wouldn't have so much fun,
would I?

The birthday boy and his bouncy castle

Next time you're on a bouncy castle, keep an eye on all the different
movements the other children are trying out. I wanted to capture these
in a poem. By the way, my next-door neighbour gave me the ending for
the poem – it actually happened to someone he knew.

Karen can jump up really high,
Steve falls down and pretends to die.
Nicola takes very small steps,
Jenny leaps then pirouettes.
Rizwan hops, slips and falls,
Sarah bounces off the walls.
Baby Mark stays near the edge,
thinks he's on a mountain ledge.
Lisa never seems to care,
somersaulting everywhere.
But me, I can't even have a go,
I broke my leg two days ago.

Christmas Eve

I often think back to my childhood when I write a poem. I used to love all the preparations for Christmas, but the days went so slowly and Christmas Eve seemed to last for ever. I just couldn't get to sleep.

I'm trying to sleep on Christmas Eve
but I really can't settle down,
and I don't want to lie
with wide open eyes
till the morning comes around.

I hear Mum and Dad downstairs,
doing their best to keep quiet,
and although I'm tucked in,
covers up to my chin,
in my head there's a terrible riot.

I'm thinking of Christmas morning
and all the presents I'll find,
but what if I've missed
something good off my list?
– it keeps going round in my mind.

We have been baking all day
making rolls, mince pies and cake,
and I know quite well
it's this heavenly smell
that's keeping me wide awake.

Perhaps I'll slip down for some water
though I ought to stay in my room,
but maybe I'll risk
a slap with the whisk
for a lick of the mixing spoon.

Now Dad says Father Christmas
won't leave any presents for me,
"Make no mistake,
if you're still awake,
he'll pass you by, you'll see!"

But I've tried and I've tried and I've tried
and I keep rolling round in my bed,
I still can't sleep,
and I'm fed up with sheep
so I'm counting reindeer instead!

Snow

Have you ever waited and waited for something to happen, and then when it did come along, been really disappointed?

This poem was written during a period of heavy snow cover which lasted for ten days. Before that, it hadn't really snowed for years, so many children didn't know what deep snow was like. I wondered how they felt.

For years and years
　　I waited for snow,
drove my family mad
　　just wanting to know,
will it snow this year,
　　will I *ever* see snow?

But now it's come
　　I just want it to go,
my fingers are frozen
　　and so are my toes.
There's an icicle formed
　　at the tip of my nose.
My ears disappeared
　　half an hour ago.
It's not like I thought:
　　how I hate this snow!

Up a tree

One Sunday afternoon I was out for a walk in a nearby park when I heard voices close by. I looked around but couldn't see anyone. Suddenly I realised that the voices were above my head. Three children were looking down at me from the branches of a tree. What were they talking about up there?

Look at us now, we're stuck up a tree,
me, my big sister and Kevin who's three,
not knowing whether to risk going down,
grey sky up above and leaves all around.

We're stuck up a tree one Sunday in June
hoping that someone comes past very soon.
I bet that we've missed something good on TV,
I wish we'd chosen an easier tree.

"I bet you can't climb it," some big lad laughed,
and none of us likes to look feeble or daft
so we tried, and we've climbed up far too high,
and I know, very soon, Kevin's going to cry.

And big sister's frozen herself to the tree,
I think she's forgotten our Kevin and me,
she's moaning softly and won't look down
and it seems like a very long drop to the ground.

Soon someone must surely pass by this tree,
some afternoon walker who'll look up and see
three frightened kids clinging desperately,
me, my big sister, and Kevin who's three.

Waving at trains

I always carry a notebook with me in which I jot down ideas, and I often work on a poem when I'm travelling by train. This is a very short poem about some children who were standing by the track. Perhaps you can hear the rhythm of the train when you read the poem aloud.

I like to wave at trains
as they hurry down the track,
but when I stick my tongue out
nobody waves back.

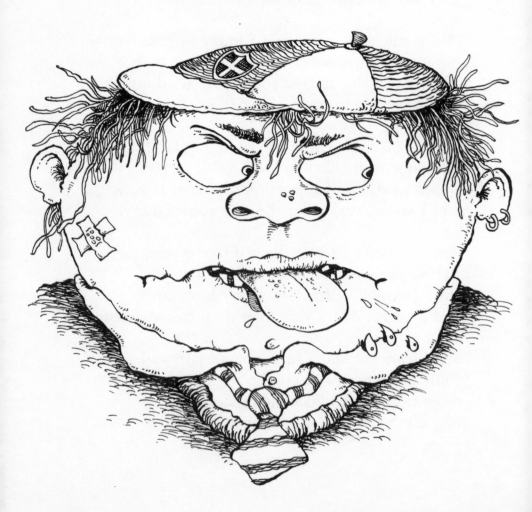

On holiday

My family and I once rented a cottage in Swanage for a week's holiday. The cottage had an attic room with a wonderful view of the sea. I called to my wife and said, "There really is a sea view . . ." and then quickly added the second line.

This is a poem to be read aloud. You could try tapping out the beat on the table as you speak.

There really is a sea view
not a see-it-if-you-jump-up-and-down view,
over the rooftops, there in the sun,
we're really having lots of fun

on holiday,
on holiday.

Torremolinos, Tenerife,
the Isle of Wight or the Barrier Reef,
whether you go to Swanage or Spain
it really doesn't matter, just hope it doesn't rain

on holiday,
on holiday.

There's a roller coaster ride by the pier
and postcards saying, "Wish you were here".
This year, next year, sunshine, NEVER!
All we need is a bit of hot weather

on holiday,
on holiday.

The noisy family rap

A rap is words spoken in time to music or some kind of background beat. I usually bang a tambour – a tambourine without bells – when I perform this piece. Children from Tollgate Junior School in Eastbourne wrote the rap with me.

Biff! Bang! Wallop and slap!
This is the noisy family rap.

The baby's always crying,
lying in her cot,
the sun's shining in
and she's getting very hot.

The kids are always arguing,
fighting over toys,
Mum's always nagging them,
fed up with the noise.

Biff! Bang! Wallop and slap!
This is the noisy family rap.

Grandad's always snoring
in his rocking chair,
Sister's always screaming,
racing down the stairs.

Dad's always hammering
nails into the wall,
I can't stand the noise
and I'm fed up with it all.

Biff! Bang! Wallop and slap!
This is the noisy family rap.

Jellyfish

Do you have favourite words? "Jellyfish" is one of mine. It has three parts to it, called syllables – *jel-ly-fish*.

I began this poem on the beach one hot summer's day. I had just rescued a stranded jellyfish and had placed it in a bucket of water. While I was watching the creature I started making up all sorts of silly rhymes to go with "jelly", and imagining all kinds of strange fish.

I think of this as a rap poem. Try saying it fast, using shakers to help you keep the beat.

Jellyfish,
jellyfish,
floats along and slaps you on the belly
fish.

Just when you thought you'd go for a swim,
just when you thought it was safe to go in.

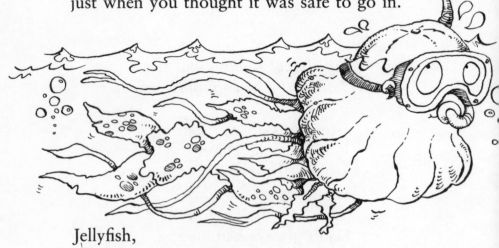

Jellyfish,
jellyfish,
saw one in a programme on the telly
fish.

Thinking about it kept me awake,
I just don't think that I can take

jellyfish,
jellyfish,
trod on one at Margate with Aunt Nelly
fish.

If you see one in the sea then give me a shout,
catch it in a bucket but keep your fingers out.

Jellyfish,
jellyfish,
odd and funny-looking umbrelly
fish,
slimy old seaside smelly
fish,

jellyfish,
jellyfish,
jellyfish,
jellyfish.

Sounds

If you read comics you will know how comic-strip artists like to play around with the shape of words. In this poem I wanted to explore how words might look if they were written the way that they sound.

Miss asked if we had any favourite sounds,
and could we quickly write them down.
Tim said the screeeeam of a mean guitar
or a saxophone or a fast sports car.
Shakira said cats when they purrrrr on your lap,
and Karen, the **CRASH!** of a thunderclap.
Paul asked what word he could possibly write
for the sound of a rocket on Guy Fawkes Night,
or a redwood tree as it fell to the ground,
and Miss said to write it as it sounds.
So Paul wrote Whoooooooooooosh with a dozen "o"s
and **CRACK** with a crack in it, just to show
the kind of noise a tree might make

as it hit the ground and made it **SHAKE** .
Then everyone called, "Hey listen to this!
What do you think? Is this right, Miss?

Do balloons go **POP!** or Bust or **BANG** ?

Do church bells **DONG** or Peeeeeal or **CLANG** ?"
Then Miss said it was quite enough
and time to stop all the silly stuff.
What she really likes, as she's often said
is a quiet room, with every head
bent over books, writing things down –
the sound of silence, her favourite sound!

Have fun with words

Now that you have read some of my poems, I'm hoping that they might spark off some ideas for your own writing. You may also like to try out some of the ideas I've suggested in this next part of the book. Not every poem has an activity to go with it. The poems I've used for activities are the ones that I have read in schools and which seem to get people talking!

When you start to plan some writing of your own, think about things that have happened to you – somewhere you've visited, perhaps, or something that has happened at school. Look around you and listen to what people say. Is there something memorable there? Sounds, sights, smells, tastes, the feel of something – ideas are everywhere and available to everyone.

Try working with a friend or two, and sharing ideas. Everyone will have something different to say about families, holidays, pets, games, school, food and all the other areas of everyday life. Talk about what you are going to write, jot down ideas, and then decide on the best.

When you are ready to begin putting ideas down on paper, don't worry about making mistakes. Write things down in any order you like. You may find that ideas come so quickly you have to write really fast. If you don't know how to spell a word, don't worry about it now, write it down as you think. It is much better to use a word you like than settle for one you're not really happy with. Experiment with your writing. Try putting words in a different order, or arranging them to make a pattern on the page. Then read what you have written to others – but maybe practise it first.

Have fun with words. I always do.

"My sister said . . ." (p. 5) and "This time" (p. 7)

Both of these poems are about the problems of getting on with one another. With brothers, sisters, parents or friends there will always be things to argue over. You might be mad with your brother because he always manages to get out of the washing up, or annoyed with your friend because she always wins any argument you have.

Try writing a poem of your own that begins "My brother said . . ." or "My cousin said . . .":

> My brother said,
> "If you don't get out of my room this minute,
> I'll put . . .
>
> mud in your milkshake,
> sand in your salad,
> talc in your treacle
> and birdseed in your butter . . .

What other threats and insults might someone come up with? Maybe it's Dad who is threatening you – even though you know he doesn't really mean a word of it!

> If you don't stop talking and get to sleep
> I'll come up there and be really mad,
> you'll wish you had someone else's dad,
> if you don't go to sleep this instant.

Michael Rosen is a poet who often writes about arguments between families or friends. Look out for his books in the library. You could also look at other poems about family life in *You Just Can't Win*, edited by Brian Moses (Blackie).

44

"Photographs" (p. 8)

Can you add to this poem? Perhaps you have family
photographs that you can look through. You might like to talk
about them with a friend and try writing a poem together. One
of you thinks of a question about the photograph while the
other tries to answer it. Start with "Who's that . . .?":

Who's that waving from the train?
That's Auntie Rose going home again.

Who's that pulling a funny face?
That's cousin Ben winning a race.

"Hippopotamus dancing" (p. 14)

Which animal would you make a beeline for if you visited a
zoo or safari park – a fox, the fish, the penguins? I wonder
what you like about the animal – is it something about the
way it looks or moves, or is it something clever that it can do?
Pair up with a friend and try to guess what each other's
favourite animal is by asking those sort of questions. Then you
could each try and put your feelings about the animal into
words:

Roo roo kangaroo,
I wish I could jump up high like you.
I wish I could . . .

Lots of poets seem to enjoy writing about animals. Have a
look at "Good morning, Mr Croco-doco-dile" by Charles
Causley in *Early in the Morning* (Puffin).

"Trouble at the Dinosaur Café" (p. 16)

Can you produce a menu for the kind of dishes that might be
served in this café? You might like to get together with some
friends and produce the Dinosaur Café Recipe Book.

```
┌─────────────────────────────────────────────┐
│ MENU                                         │
│                                              │
│ Portions for baby dinosaurs                  │
│ Mixed leaves with slices of tree bark        │
│ Twig twiglets                                │
│ Marsh grass with swamp dressing              │
│ Pond weed soup                               │
└─────────────────────────────────────────────┘
```

"The grumposaurus" (p. 18)

Have you ever imagined that your little sister or baby brother
might be a noisydactyl or a messyodocus? What would these
creatures look like? Can you think of suitable names for other
members of your family, or for friends, or teachers? Try
writing about them as dinosaurs:

> The noisydactyl
> roars about the house,
> howls out for her Mum
> and bellows, "Where's my teddy?"

"First and last" (p. 27)

Can you think of other opposites which would work in a
poem? Instead of first and last, try best and worst. You could
also try writing about somebody else instead of yourself – your
mum, your dog, your friend:

> You're the best at painting
> but the worst at clearing up.
> You're the best talker
> but the worst listener . . .

"Well, what happened?" (p. 28)

Could you write a poem or a conversation for two voices?
Think of other times when two children might explain things
differently. Perhaps the classroom hamster has escaped and the

teacher wants to know what happened.

> It wasn't me,
> I didn't let him out.
> It was Lindsey,
> she's the one you should clout!

Other situations might include an argument on a bus where the driver thinks two children are trying to travel free, or in the swimming pool where someone has just been pushed into the water, or at home over who reads the comic first.

"On holiday" (p. 37)
and "The noisy family rap" (p. 38)

To get the feel of a rap poem, it might be a good idea to practise performing these two poems – perhaps in a group. Like some pieces of music, rap poems have a strong rhythm – just listen and follow! If you've ever heard rap, you'll know that it's never quiet and shy; the poems need to be said boldly and clearly against a background beat. This could be a piece of music which suits the poem, or – more simply – a percussion beat with beaters, shakers, drums and so on. You will need to find somewhere to practise, and it's a good idea to take a tape recorder with you so that you can listen to your performance and maybe improve it. Then you could perform it to your class.

The next stage is to try to write a rap yourself, or with a friend, or maybe the whole class could write a class rap:

> Biff! Bang! Wallop and slap!
> This is the noisy Class 4 rap.

"Jellyfish" (p. 40)

Like the rap poems "On holiday" (p. 37) and "The noisy
family rap" (p. 38), this poem has a strong rhythm which
carries you along. Just like music, certain lines have a
foot-tapping beat. Why not try to perform it?

Longer words – with a number of parts – have a rhythm of
their own. The word "jel-ly-fish" has three parts to it, called
syllables, which makes it a good word to say – a satisfying
mouthful! You could try to write a poem of your own using a
three-syllable word like tram-po-line, roll-er-skates, or
un-der-ground:

> Underground, underground,
> rats and moles live underground,
> that is where they're to be found,
> underground, underground.

"Sounds" (p. 42)

Can you think of any other sounds you could "write"? Most of
the sounds in my poem are noisy ones. What about some
quieter ones? You could try to illustrate a few.

Some words can be written in such a clever way that their
letters form a picture of the word's meaning:

What words are these? Can you think of any others of your
own?